THE OBJECT LESSON

THE OBJECT LESSON

THE REVEREND NEHEMIAH PROPHET

© 2025 all rights reserved

GRANO SALAS PUBLISHERS
EUREKA, CALIFORNIA

ISBN: 978-7333784-1-3
LCCN: 2025945038

Library of Congress-In-Publication Data has been applied for

Once your mind contains no plan
wherever you are its alert.
          - Hanshan

If you can rid yourself of conceptual thought,
you will have accomplished everything.
          - Huang Po

Somewhere something incredible
 is waiting to happen.
          - John Archibald Wheeler

    Dancia Ephemera awoke with a start,
"Alas, alack! Whence did I come?
Whithersoever shall I go?
But a mortal coil is this morsel of clay -
and what of so much pointless
inconsequence? - this then is life."

    It didn't think much of its name either:
"It has less substance than a soap bubble.
Why not Maximus? Victor? Constant even?
Let it be any other name. What were they
 thinking?" The name would pale in light
of a slightly more pressing concern -

It was late in
 the morning before

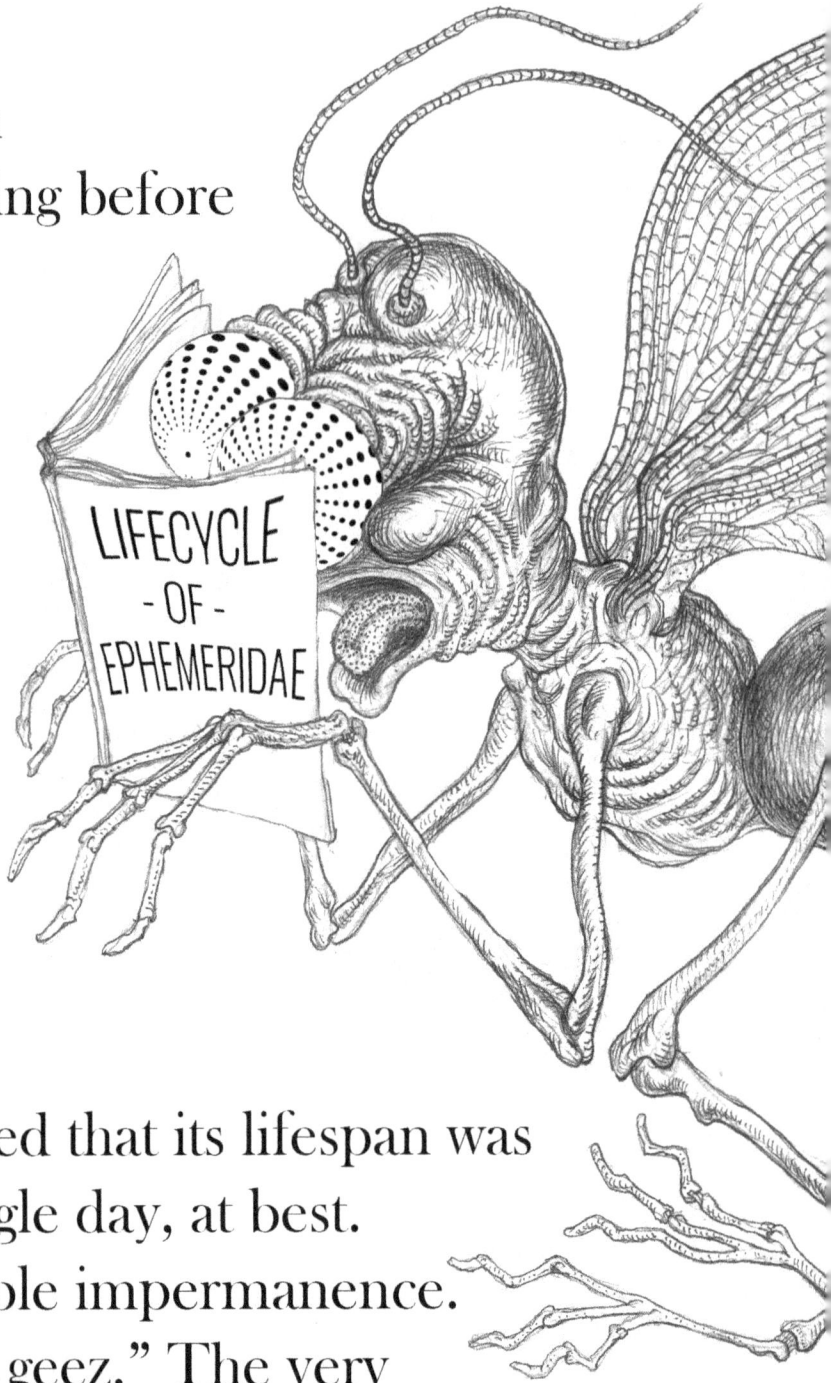

LIFECYCLE
- OF -
EPHEMERIDAE

Dancia realized that its lifespan was
 fixed at a single day, at best.
"What palpable impermanence.
It's so unfair, geez." The very
thought stole its breath.
"Wha happen?".
 No time to fret, never mind a crisis . . .
  out of the question.

"Get a hold of yourself.
Think fast. Think big.
What is of real importance?
Above all, what is decisively
and unassailably 'of essence'
in the scheme
of things?"

"What precisely
in life is that
which matters?"

"Should I give in to every cell of my
basal ganglia screaming, 'What the
world needs now is more of me, me, me'.
"Spread thy genes thither and yon. Make
for thyself a rapt fanbase, a bona fide,
sure-fire raison d'être; the delight of
midlife; the protection and succor
of my golden years. . . and I could be
the pride of my parents, at long last,
it dreamed." Abandoned to every impulse
of its imagination, Dancia raved, "Waste
no time. Make a whole swarm of me
to mourn and grieve my absence -
my portrait upon a thousand nightstands,
countless copies of my genes,
recombining ad infinitum,
unto oblivion, ha!
Wait until they get a load of Ephemera",
"But, wait! What about me?

Do I really want to be laying around on my deathbed, plagued with the regret that I did not apply myself consistently enough to get my kicks in? I've got to get it all in, man." "I must really haunt the carnivals and get a great bang out of the doings. I have to ride every ride into the ground. Master every picayune game on the everlasting midway. I shall whack every mole, shoot every duck, shoot the works, go for broke, hit the jackpot, win the bullseye kewpie and the giant plush toy.Get scammed? Maybe, but scam them right back, only twice as hard. Who among you dare lay odds against a juggernaut? Otherwise, what is the point of this miserable toil?"

AMAZING

SUPER FREAK

SUPER FREAK

GO TO NEPTILE
EATS AS IT GROWS

THE
BIG MAN

HE IS YOU

"Wait a minute . . . too trivial. It is substance that matters. I am nothing, if not substantial. Would it be better that I make the grand tour? Girdle the globe? Think about it: Me, a globe-trotting, jet-set insect about the world. No, rather imagine me: a rambling, gambling, thoroughly jaded insect about town, having been around the block enough to have no use for other insects - having known them and knowing everything there is to know about them. Meditating instead, upon the state of the world and the various branches of knowledge: ontology, epistemology, ethics and so forth. This strikes me as somehow consequential."

"Come to think of it, maybe vanquishing the vanishing geological features would be the more constructive use of time. Consider glaciers, for instance. Should I observe endangered species in captivity? Insitu? Gorillas? Hmm, no, both the endangered species and endangered habitat in one go: I'll swim with the manatees in what's left of the coral reefs, impressive, hmm. Better yet, lemurs in their pathetic rainforest.
Too morbid . . . What, am I a ghoul? No, I'll save the rainforest. I'll create a Ponzi scheme to save the - whoa! I could be THAT Insect."
That's it. I'll call it the, 'Keep the Amazon Amazing Foundation'. I'll corral the cattle barons. I'll cut the timber empire down to size.

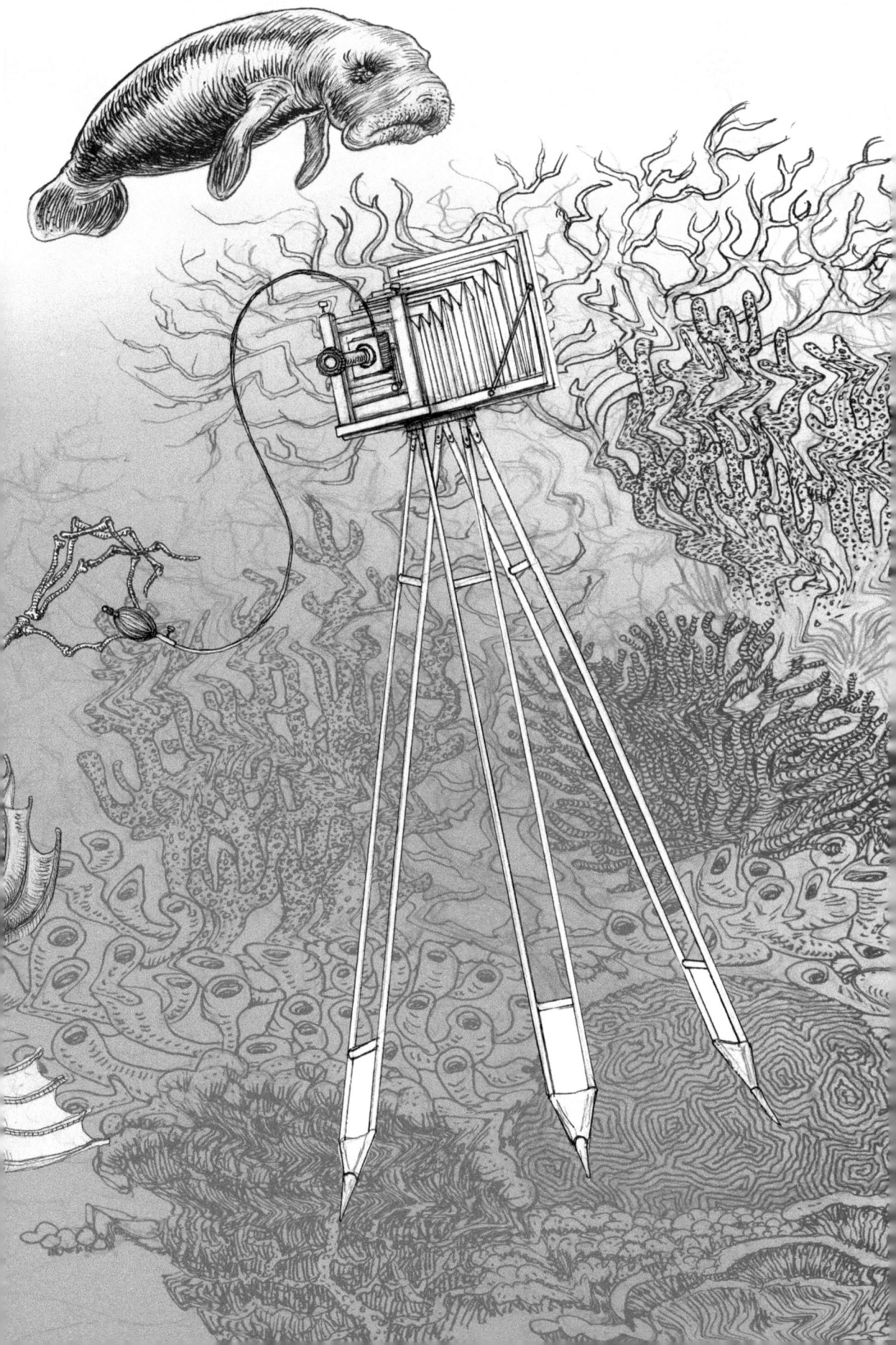

"That could never be me.
I'm a rugged individualist.
I don't play to the crowd.
I've got it.
A composer of symphonies,
who is also a concert virtuoso
while yet not above
bowing magnanimously
to thundering applause.
Shrieks, whistles, hisses, moans,
involuntary ejaculations, just imagine,
love me, hate me, whatever,
my emotional
depth shall not be denied."

"But, what if all of the low-hanging fruit has been taken? What if I can't summon a muse to surpass Mozart's Jupiter, even? What - me, simply derivative? – worse, my excruciatingly wrought oeuvre a pastiche? Shucks! And what if my virtuosity should require some singular ability? And what if I should not possess said ability? In that case I guess I'll just have to write a song that will be for the ages, meaning a red-hot radio single. Let's see. . .danceable yet pithy, with a series of irresistible hooks that will hijack the brain with the focus and urgency of an unquenchable earwig."

Woah, over the top. A brilliant legal mind?
A gifted surgeon? This is it - a billionaire!
Knockin' it down and saltin' it away
– yes this defines who I am.

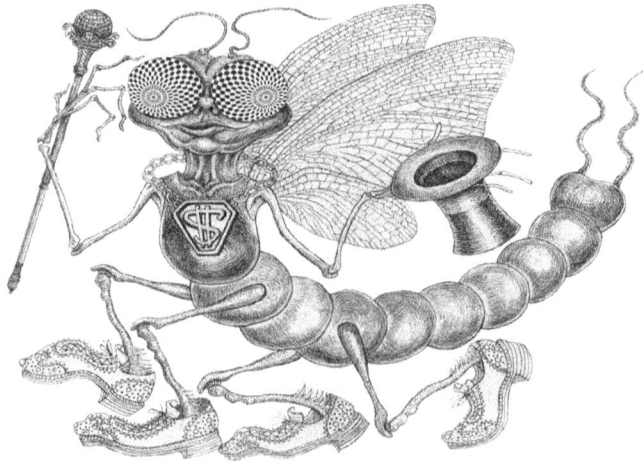

. . . a rich and famous public defender.
No . . . I've got it! The summation, the
embodiment, and destiny of my very
being here and now: a rich, famous
athlete! That's it, I'll dunk it in their face
and snag for myself the biggest salary and
the most generous product endorsements
heretofore amassed by an unrestricted
free agent. Oh yes, Ephemera will
break all of these lousy records
once and for all."

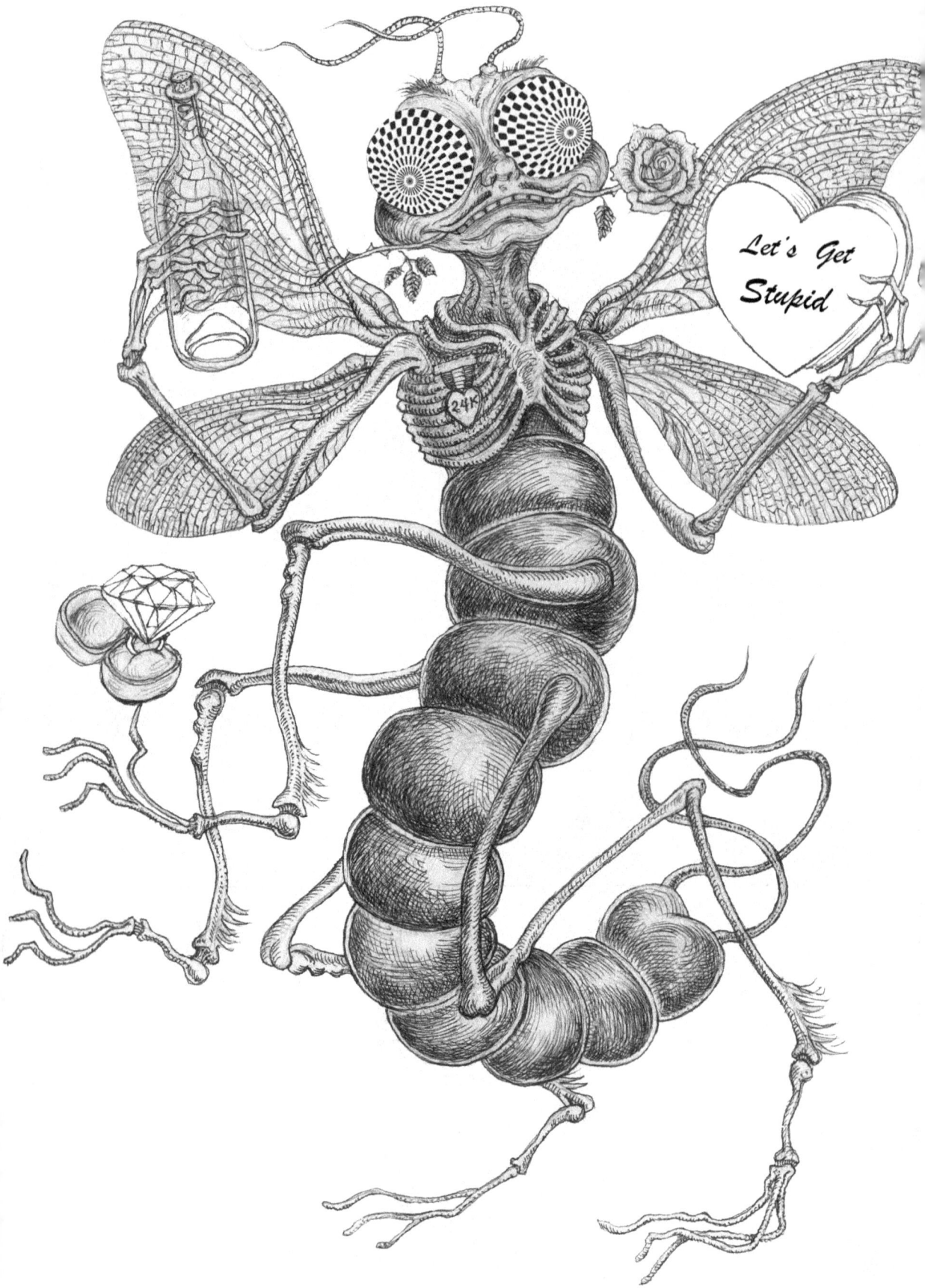

Let's Get Stupid

"Records? Who cares about records? The deeper I go the more apparent it becomes that I should spend my one life breaking hearts and striking rare-earth minerals with every new romance. Ooh-wee! Eat your hearts out you pathetic wallflowers. Make way for Don Juan Dancia. Me? Oh yes, why not? What ever can it be that is so appealing, so satisfying, so habit-forming about this singular fly? Hmm . . . Truth is a cold abyss, losers."

Vanity, I know thy name.
Should I practice abstinence?
Verily, shall I wield a millstone
about my neck? Scourge my scruples?
Don a scanty tunic? A bamboo raincoat
and an umbrella hat? A lousy hair shirt?
Mortify my flesh with a cat o'nine tails,
for the love of God?"
Thus Dancia perseverated late into
the afternoon. It was getting toward
evening when the dazzling chariot
of Phoebus was making its descent toward
a final blaze. Dancia, wracked with guilt
and flummoxed asunder;
having speculated its life away,
and for all that, not one step closer to
realizing any purpose whatsoever -
destined to be one of the numbers,
never having made its mark.
"A meaningless life, a nobody
- a nonentity."

Dancia grew impassive. "Should I squeeze what's left of this momentary chance awareness into a final nostalgic reverie or kick back and anticipate a grim diminishing future?
- the mind reels."
"Now that I have the benefit of perspective, I wish that I could turn back time to when I was thinking about how I was going to be the big-time gamer on the carnival circuit", it reminisced wistfully, "Life was so full of possibility then. Everything seemed entirely within reach".

At length, Dancia withdrew and beelined for a wooded vale, ambiguously concealing a derelict temple in the act of submerging itself into a primeval pond, the depth of which was liable to be mistaken for sheer nothingness. There, it happened upon Astrochelys Radiata, living the contemplative life in seclusion.

The sum of the exchange was to the following effect:

Dancia: Your reverence, learned adept,
 noble anchorite, have I lived my life
all wrong?

Radiata: You came to the right spacetime,
novice. Are you aware of the fact that I
have lived an astonishing 188 years?
Or what would be . . . notice to wit,
the way that I can do this sort of math
 in my head . . . let's see . . . 373, 249
of your estimated lifetimes?

Dancia: Ariiight your excellence,
 I can't say that I was, but thanks.

Radiata: Imagine, if you are even capable,
 the disparity of our relative acumen,
just think.

Dancia: Come on, I'm hep. Fahhh out.

Radiata: Are you aware that my binomial
 literally means Radiant Star Tortoise?
Brilliant cynosure surrounded by a
common firmament of lesser lights.
Is it my fault if I'm a charismatic
megafauna over here? - if you can dig.

Dancia: Dig, but I would have thought
that the name might have referred to the
radiating streaks on your shell, resembling
dappled light on a forest floor, conferred
 by natural selection acting on eons of
genetic variation?

Radiata: Well in that case, you would
have been wrong. It's my name.
 So, what is your problem?

Dancia: I fail to comprehend the slightest
 meaning of life in the least. As far as I can
tell, life has no point or destination.
Nothing to realize and neither
 jot nor tittle to lay hold of.

Radiata: Poore inch of nature. And?

Dancia: Am I a heretic? An infidel? Should
I expect to end as a speck of carbon in
The Lake of Fire?

Radiata: Pray art thee accountable for
thy mischief?

Dancia: For a mayfly? Come on, man.

Radiata: Who then has returned from that
undiscovered country? Over and above,
who knows what dreams may come?

Dancia: I am talking about this life - my life.
The thing that gets under my craw is
missing out on purpose. If I had a purpose,
the meaning might have been obvious.

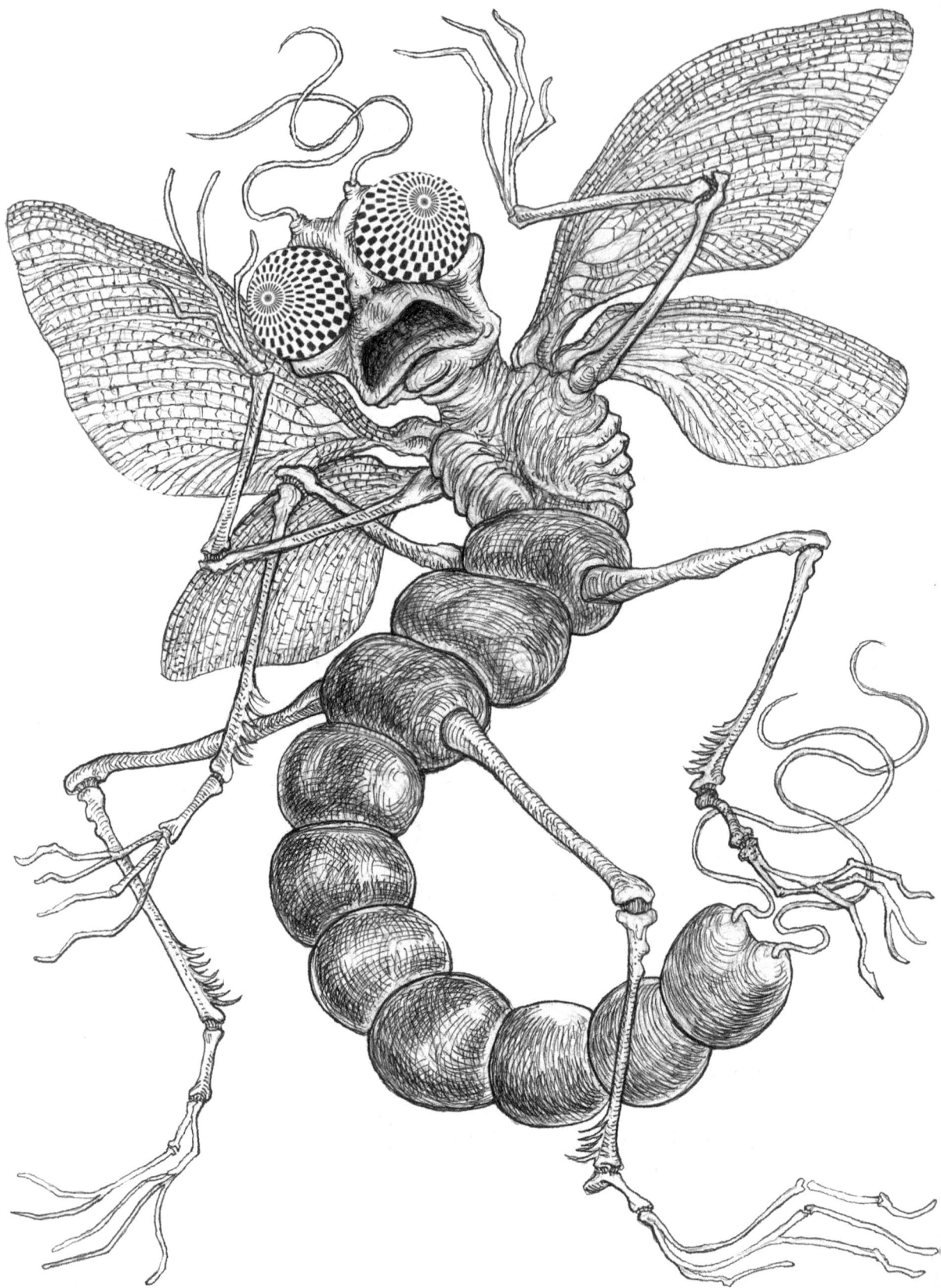

Radiata: Nonsense! Thou art a common insect of a thing, a prop, a cautionary tale, an object lesson, yet another teensy reminder that the sands are numbered, and delays have dangerous ends.

Dancia: Oh great, thanks. Still though, what about meaning? At the very least there must be some meaning to all of this moronic futility.

Radiata: It is a tale told by an idiot signifying not one iota. 188 years of continuous prosperity is but another dance upon the grave.

Dancia: Perhaps life is lived more fully in as much as it has no meaning?

Radiata: Who cares? You have wasted time and time doth waste you.

Dancia: Well then, who cares about what ends delays have? Or, about the number of sands for that matter.

Radiata: Et tu, novice? Thou hast spoke too much already, get the gone.

Accordingly, Dancia bugged off.

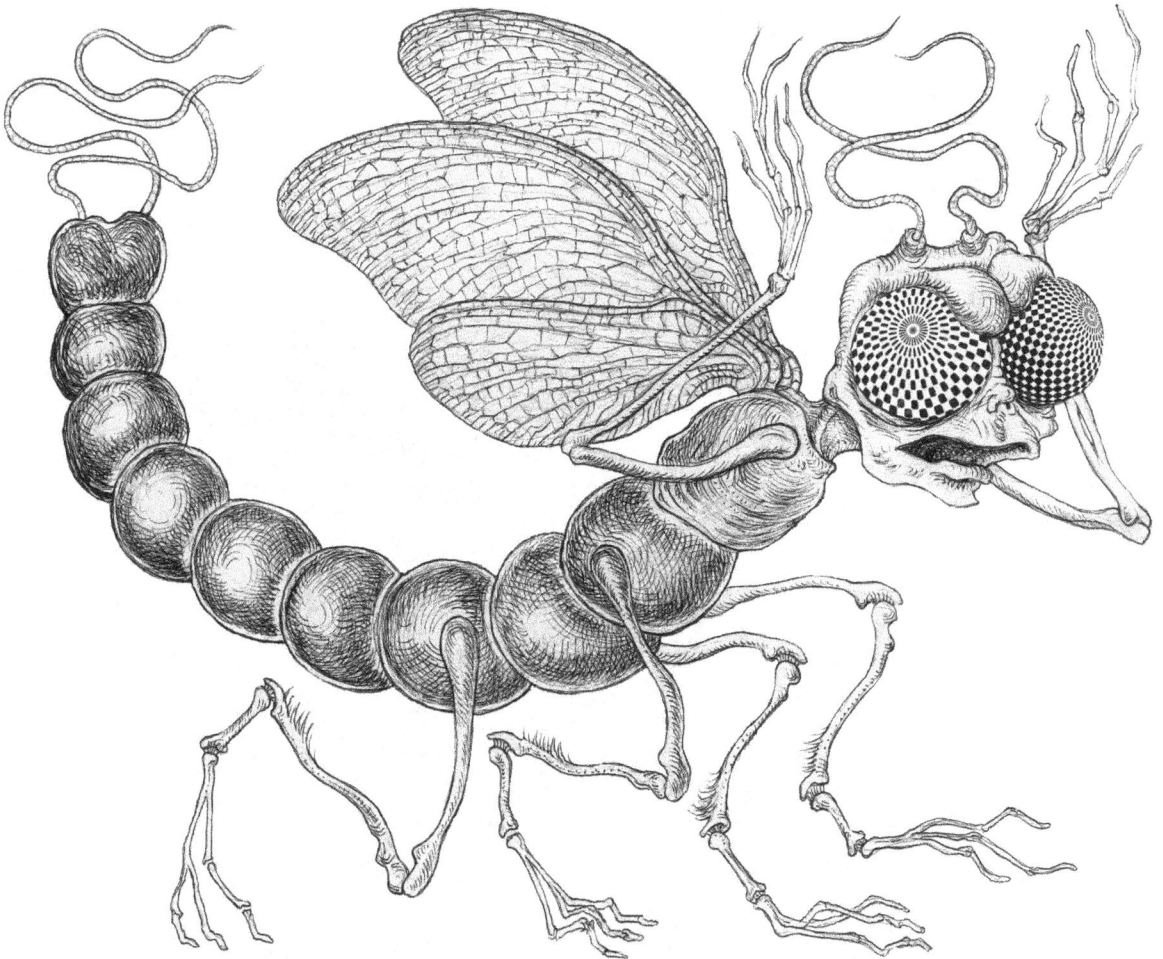

It was then that Dancia descried a full-blown lotus appearing to beg the day for mercy, "Could it be that meaning is observer dependent?" In an instant it discovered itself in a superposition state. The boundary between things seen and unseen fell away. Dancing to the beat of its own arrythmia, timelessness and nowhere shuffled into infinity. In experiencing its expression in its present reality, actor became the action, subject became object, inhered in the act of living into the shadow of the setting Sun.

The rest was silence.

www.ingramcontent.com/pod-product-compliance
Lightning Source LLC
Chambersburg PA
CBHW081242020426
42331CB00013B/3267